D1366151

Mountains

KINGFISHER
LONDON & NEW YORK

First published as *Kingfisher Young Knowledge: Mountains* in 2007
Additional material produced for Macmillan Children's Books by Discovery Books Ltd.
Library of Congress Cataloging-in-Publication data has been applied for.

ISBN: 978-0-7534-6835-7

Kingfisher books are available for special promotions and premiums. For details contact:
Special Markets Department, Macmillan, 175 Fifth Ave., New York, NY 10010.

For more information, please visit www.kingfisherbooks.com

Printed in China
1 3 5 7 9 8 6 4 2
1TR/0512/UTD/WKT/140MA

Note to readers: the website addresses listed in this book are correct at the time of going to print. However, due to the ever-changing nature of the Internet, website addresses and content can change. Websites can contain links that are unsuitable for children. The publisher cannot be held responsible for changes in website addresses or content or for information obtained through a third party. We strongly advise that Internet searches are supervised by an adult.

Acknowledgments
The publisher would like to thank the following for permission to reproduce their material. Every care has been taken to trace copyright holders. However, if there have been unintentional omissions or failure to trace copyright holders, we apologize and will, if informed, endeavor to make corrections in any future edition.
b = bottom, *c* = center, *l* = left, *t* = top, *r* = right

Photographs: cover all images courtesy of Shutterstock.com; 1 Corbis/W. Wayne Lockwood; 2–3 Corbis/Charlie Munsey; 4–5 Alamy/Nagelestock; 6–7 Corbis/Eye Ubiquitous; 7*tr* Corbis/Galen Rowell; 9 Shutterstock Images/fpolat; 10–11 Photolibrary.com; 11*br* Getty/Science Faction; 12 Corbis/Joseph Sohm; 13 Corbis/Ric Ergenbright; 15*tr* Frank Lane Picture Agency/Winfried Wisniewski; 15*bl* Arboretum de Villardebelle, France; 16–17 Getty/Stone; 17*br* Alamy/Aflo Foto; 18*l* Corbis/Galen Rowell; 18–19 Getty/Imagebank; 19*r* Photolibrary.com; 20 Corbis/Eye Ubiquitous; 21*t* Corbis/Tom Bean; 21*br* Corbis/Paul A. Souders; 22 Alamy/Brett Baunton; 23*t* Natural History Picture Agency/Alberto Nardi; 23*b* Science Photo Library/Kaj R. Svensson; 24 Corbis/Steve Kaufman; 25*t* Alamy/Imagina Photography; 25*b* Corbis/Joe McDonald; 26*c* Alamy/Andrew Woodley; 26–27*b* Getty/Stone; 27*t* Alamy/Terry Fincher Photos; 28–29 Photolibrary.com; 29*t* Alamy/Mediacolor's; 30 Corbis/Zefa; 31*t* Getty/Photographer's Choice; 31*br* Getty/Aurora; 32 Getty/Digital Vision; 33*tl* Alamy/David R. Frazier Photolibrary; 33*b* Alamy/Phototake; 34 Alamy/Publiphoto Diffusion; 35*tl* John Cleare Mountain Camera; 35*b* Getty/Photographer's Choice; 36*c* Royal Geographical Society; 36*br* Corbis Montagne Magazine; 37 Corbis/Sygma; 38 Alamy/f1 online; 38–39 Alamy/StockShot; 39*c* Corbis/Ashley Cooper; 40 Corbis/EPA; 41*t* Corbis/John van Hasselt; 41*b* Frank Lane Picture Agency/Foto Natura; 43*tl* Getty/NGS; 43*b* Mary Evans Picture Library; 48 Shutterstock Images/Ricardo Manuel Silva de Sousa; 49*t* Shutterstock Images/steve100; 49*b* Shutterstock Images/Galyna Andrushko; 52 Shutterstock Images/Sam D. Cruz; 53*bl* Shutterstock Images/Luigi Nifosi; 53*br* Shutterstock Images/Vulkanette; 56 Shutterstock Images/hipproductions

Illustrations on pages: 8, 11, 12, 13, 16 Peter Winfield; 14–15 Steve Weston

Commissioned photography on pages 44–47 by Andy Crawford
Thank you to models Jamie Chang-Leng, Mary Conquest, and Georgina Page

Mountains

Margaret Hynes

KINGFISHER
NEW YORK

Contents

What are mountains?

A mountain is a giant steep-sided rock that rises above Earth's surface. There are mountains on land, under the oceans, and even on other planets.

Mighty mountain ranges

A group of mountains is called a range. The Himalayas is a mountain range in Asia. It is home to the world's highest peaks.

Cold at the top

There is less—or thinner—air at the top of a mountain than there is at the bottom. It is also colder, so some peaks are snowy all year long.

Moving world

Earth's rocky surface is called the crust. It is divided into plates that fit together like a jigsaw puzzle. The plates move very slowly over the face of the Earth.

Moving plates

This map shows the plates and the direction in which they are moving. Some plates crash into each other, while others pull apart.

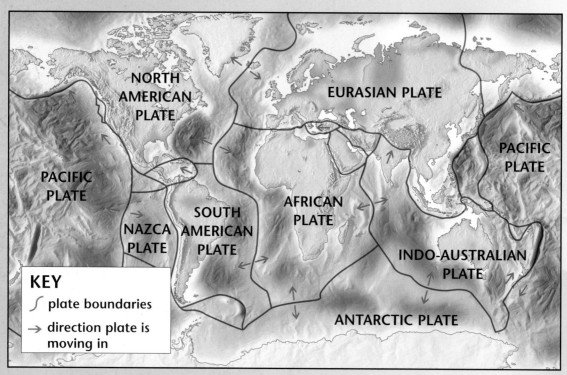

NORTH AMERICAN PLATE

EURASIAN PLATE

PACIFIC PLATE

PACIFIC PLATE

AFRICAN PLATE

NAZCA PLATE

SOUTH AMERICAN PLATE

INDO-AUSTRALIAN PLATE

ANTARCTIC PLATE

KEY

〰 plate boundaries

→ direction plate is moving in

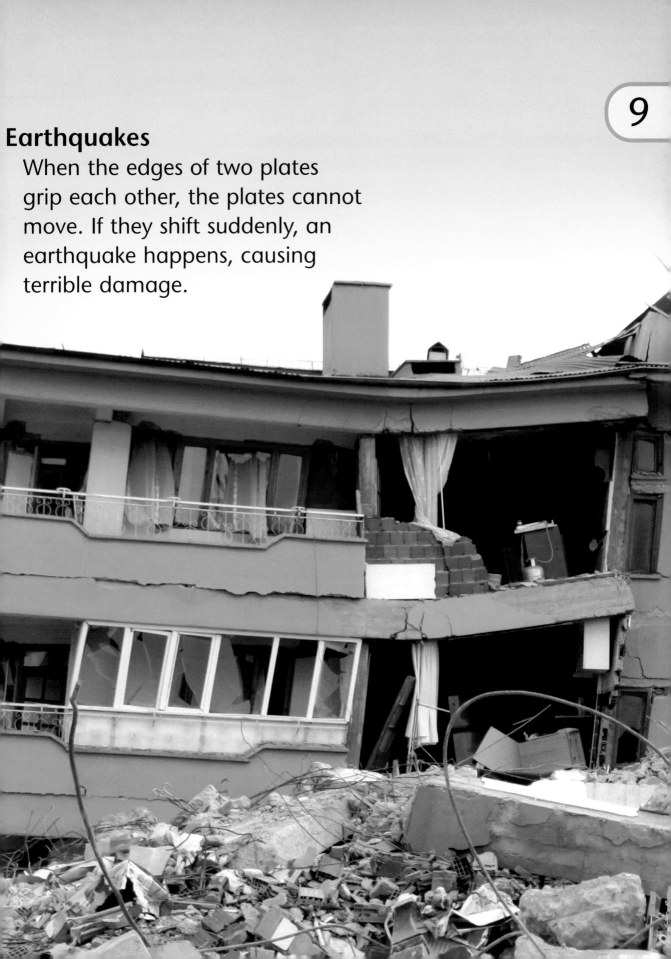

Earthquakes

When the edges of two plates grip each other, the plates cannot move. If they shift suddenly, an earthquake happens, causing terrible damage.

Mountains of fire

Some mountains are volcanoes. They form when hot, melted rock called magma erupts from a crack in Earth's crust. The liquid rock cools and hardens into a mountain.

Violent eruption
Mount Etna is a volcano in Italy. When it erupts, magma bursts out. Ash, gas, steam, and hot rock shoot into the sky.

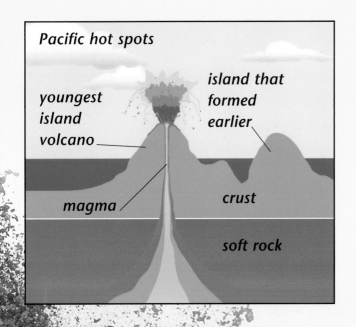

Pacific hot spots

youngest island volcano

island that formed earlier

magma

crust

soft rock

Hot spots

The Hawaiian Islands are volcanoes. They form as the Pacific plate passes over a hot and active area under Earth's crust called a hot spot.

Flowing lava

Once magma pours out of a volcano, it is called lava. It rolls downhill like a river of fire.

Rising rock

Many mountains form in areas where plates push against each other. The moving plates squeeze the land up, creating mountains.

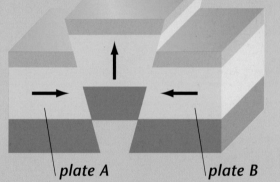

squeezing action pushes up blocks of rock

plate A

plate B

Fault-block mountains

The moving plates can cause cracks in the crust. These break the crust into blocks, and some rise up to form fault-block mountains.

Rounded off

The Wasatch Range in Utah is a fault-block mountain range. Its blocky shape has been worn down over time.

Fold mountains

When two plates crash together, they can cause layers of rock in the crust to buckle and rise. This forms fold mountains.

valley

mountain

continent A crashes into continent B

continent B

Folding rock

As the layers of rock in the crust are squashed, they form zigzagging shapes called folds.

On a mountainside

A high mountain has several zones, or regions. Each zone has different plants and animals. Very few plants or animals live near the top.

Plant cover

Forests cover this mountain's lower region. Farther up is a zone of small low-lying plants called alpines.

conifers

deciduous trees

icy peak

alpine region

Mountain birds

The wind is so strong at the top of mountains that only powerful birds, such as this lammergeier, can fly there.

Conifers

These cones and pine needles belong to the spruce conifer. Conifer trees have a triangular shape. This helps the snow slide off them.

Mountain weather

The weather can change very quickly on mountains. A storm can start in just a few minutes. The temperature can quickly drop to below freezing.

Rain shelter

Some mountains are so high that they block rain clouds. One slope may be rainy while the other side stays dry.

rain clouds

dry desert

lush vegetation

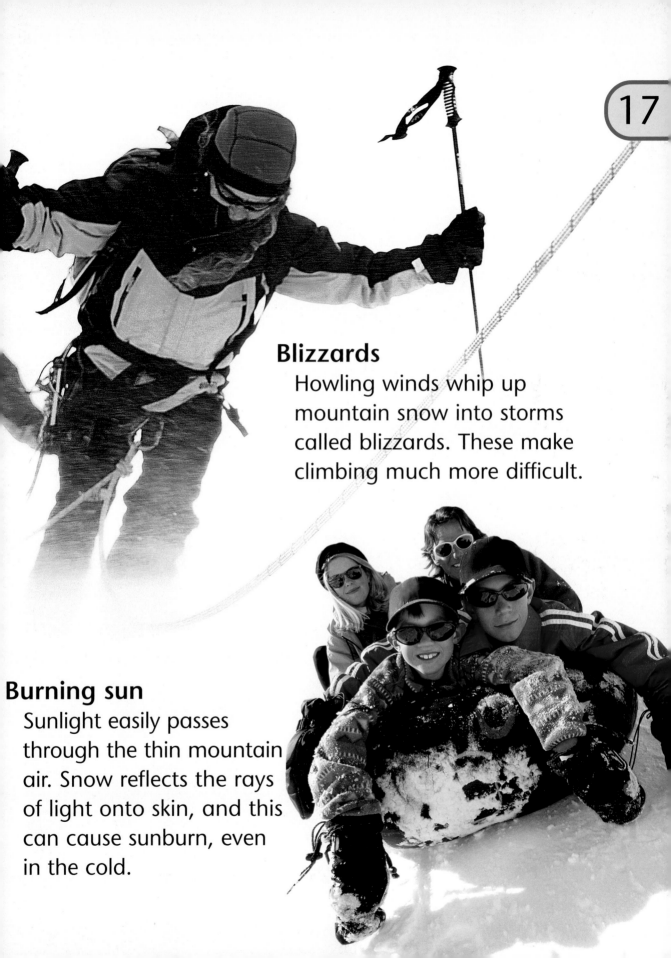

Blizzards

Howling winds whip up
mountain snow into storms
called blizzards. These make
climbing much more difficult.

Burning sun

Sunlight easily passes
through the thin mountain
air. Snow reflects the rays
of light onto skin, and this
can cause sunburn, even
in the cold.

Glaciers

Huge rivers of ice called glaciers form on the peaks of some of the world's highest mountains. Glaciers move downhill very slowly.

How glaciers form
Snow collects in rocky hollows called cirques high up a mountain. The snow turns into ice and forms a glacier.

Cracks in the ice

Cracks called crevasses form in a glacier as it moves over bumpy ground. Crevasses are very deep and dangerous, so climbers use safety ropes.

Left behind

Glaciers pick up rubble and drag it along with them. When the ice melts, these rocks are left behind.

Wear and tear

All mountains are under attack from the elements. Ice, wind, and running water slowly wear them down over millions of years.

Old mountain

A young mountain is jagged. As it gets older, the elements slowly wear it down, and it becomes more rounded.

Ice sculptures

As a glacier creeps along,
it scrapes a mountainside.
Eventually, it gouges out huge
U-shaped valleys, such as this
one in California.

Rolling rocks

Ice breaks away small
rocks from this mountain.
These tumble down the
slope and gather in
a pile at the bottom.

Plucky plants

Plants that grow high up on mountain slopes have adapted to cope with the biting cold, fierce winds, and freezing weather there.

Tiny trees

Some willow and birch trees grow high up on mountainsides. They avoid the howling winds by hugging the ground.

Alpine snowbell

The alpine snowbell gives off heat that melts the snow around it. The plant's heat enables it to bloom in the spring.

Growing on rocks

Lichens live on rocky peaks. They form acids that make rocks crumble. Then they send tiny roots into the rocks to suck up any nutrients in them.

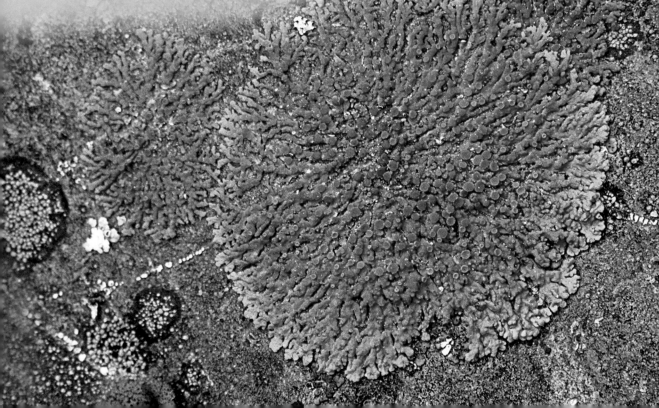

Adaptable animals

Some animals that live on mountains have adapted to cope with the steep slopes. Others have adapted to living with high winds and freezing conditions.

Hot bath

Japanese macaque monkeys wallow in hot pools during cold winters. The water is heated by volcanoes.

Mountain climber

Mountain goats are good at scrambling over rocky mountain faces. Their hooves are hollow and act like suction pads, helping the goats grip.

Natural antifreeze

The Yarrow's spiny lizard's blood stays liquid in temperatures below freezing, so it can survive on icy peaks in Mexico.

Living on mountains

Mountain peoples have learned how to live in steep, remote, and sometimes dangerous places. They grow crops for food and raise animals there.

Mountain animals

Yaks are useful animals. They provide farmers with food and wool. They are also used to carry goods.

Mountain cities

Kathmandu, Nepal, nestles in the Himalayas. It has the same facilities as any other modern city.

Growing food

Mountain fields are steep, and there is not much soil. Many farmers build terraces to stop the soil from washing away.

Going places

It can be difficult to travel on mountains because they are very steep. People have come up with clever ways for making mountain travel easier.

Long and winding roads

Mountain roads do not follow a straight line because they would be too steep to climb. The roads take a zigzagging route instead.

Climbing on a cable

A moving cable pulls this cable car between stations at the top and bottom of a mountain. Skiers use cable cars to get to snow high up on mountains.

Tourism

Mountains are great places to explore and enjoy. People can ski, hike, climb, or mountain bike along the steep slopes. But we must protect these places so that everyone can enjoy them in the future.

Jumping off

Hang gliders jump off mountaintops to float down on their gliders' wings. They glide on the warm air that rises from the ground.

Winter sports

Skiers and snowboarders love snow-covered mountains. They can slide and jump down the slippery slopes.

Mountain of trash

Many tourists drop their trash during mountain visits. This pollutes the area and can harm the wildlife that lives there.

Mountain resources

Hidden inside mountains lie valuable resources, such as building materials and metals. There are also useful resources on the slopes, such as trees.

Building blocks

Each day, big dump trucks remove tons of rock and rubble from mountains. These are used to make buildings and bridges.

Cutting down trees

Logging companies plant fast-growing trees on mountainsides. When the trees have grown, loggers cut them down for timber and fuel.

Mining metals

Some mountain rocks are rich in gold, silver, copper, and tin. Miners use large drills to dig these metals out of the stone.

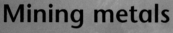

Mountaineering today

Today's mountaineers are well prepared for their climbs. They have special food for energy, layers of clothing for warmth, and lots of safety equipment.

A good night's sleep
Mountaineers shelter in tents at night and in bad weather. The tents are lightweight, strong, and waterproof.

Oxygen supply
Climbers carry tanks of oxygen that they use to help them breathe more easily in the thin mountain air.

Climbing suit
Climbers wear one-piece suits filled with down for warmth. A suit is windproof and waterproof.

Reaching the top

Mountain climbing is a popular sport. Many people have now climbed even the highest mountains, including the tallest on land, Mount Everest.

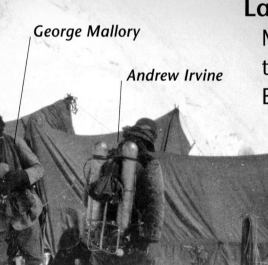

George Mallory

Andrew Irvine

Last climb

Mallory and Irvine began to climb Everest in 1924. Both men died on the mountain, but no one knows if they reached the top before they died.

Extraordinary climber

Reinhold Messner has climbed the world's 14 highest peaks. He was the first person to climb Everest without extra oxygen.

Wonder woman
Catherine Destivelle is a world-class climber. She tackles dangerous slopes and often uses only one or two of her fingers to pull herself upward.

Avalanche!

A large mass of snow and ice can suddenly break loose and crash down a mountainside. This is called an avalanche.

Predicting avalanches

Scientists use information gathered in weather stations like this one to help them predict when avalanches are likely.

Avalanche in action

Some avalanches can move as fast as a racecar. They sweep away everything in their path, including trees, people, and even villages.

Protection

This steel fence has been built to stop an avalanche from reaching the town farther downhill. It will slow down an avalanche.

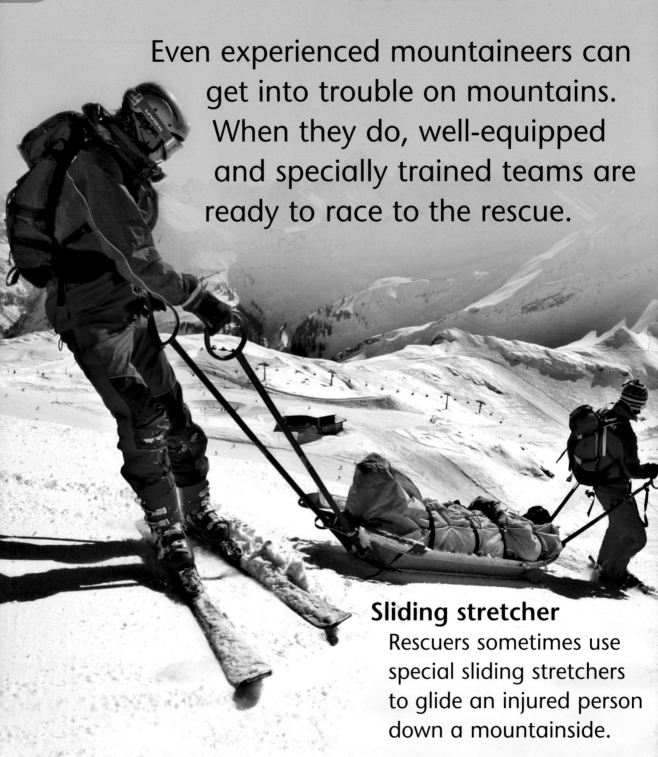

Mountain rescue

Even experienced mountaineers can get into trouble on mountains. When they do, well-equipped and specially trained teams are ready to race to the rescue.

Sliding stretcher
Rescuers sometimes use special sliding stretchers to glide an injured person down a mountainside.

Helicopter rescue

Helicopters can quickly reach remote peaks. Rescuers can then help the injured people and take them to the hospital.

Rescue dog

St. Bernard dogs have a strong sense of smell. They can be specially trained to sniff out the victims of avalanches.

Mountain mysteries

People sometimes see strange things when they climb a mountain. They might find fossil fish or they might be followed by a huge shadow.

Ghostly shadow

If someone climbs a mountain when the sun is low, the sun casts an enormous shadow on any low clouds.

Something fishy

People often find fossil fish in rocks in fold mountains. Millions of years ago, these mountains were part of the seabed.

Bigfoot

Some people believe a large creature named Bigfoot roams the Rocky Mountains in North America. No one knows if it actually exists.

Making mountains

Make a fold mountain range

Discover how land is forced upward when two plates collide by doing this simple experiment.

Roll out each ball of clay to make a rough square 1 in. (25mm) thick.

You will need:
- 2 balls of modeling clay, different colors
- Tray
- Rolling pin
- Plastic wrap

Lay both pieces 0.5 in. (10mm) apart on the plastic wrap on top of the tray.

Gently push the two clay blocks together. Your mountain range will rise upward.

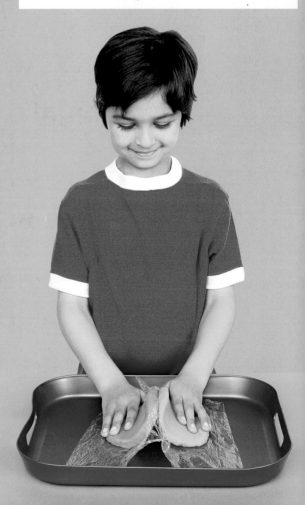

Leaving footprints

Bigfoot's calling card

Bigfoot's footprints are called its "calling card." Make one to give to a friend.

You will need:
- Large pieces of card stock
- Paints and paintbrush
- Markers
- Scissors
- Sponge

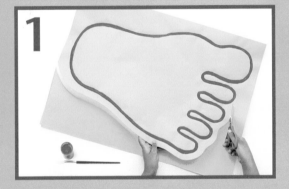

Fold the card in half, then paint a big foot shape. Cut out the shape, but do not cut the folded side.

On a sponge, draw a smaller foot shape. Cut this out.

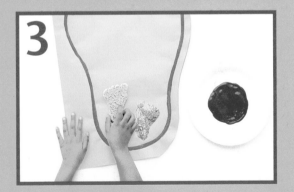

Dip the sponge in some paint and decorate your foot with lots of small footprints walking up toward the toes.

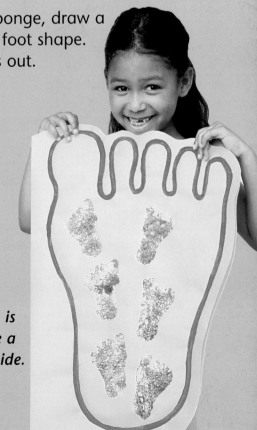

Your giant calling card is ready. Write a message inside.

Moving cable car

Make a cable car

Cable cars can climb high mountains on moving cables. Make a model with stations at the top and bottom of your mountain range.

You will need:

- 3 small cereal boxes
- Colored paper
- Sticky tape
- Sharp pencil
- Modeling clay
- 1 long, 1 short piece of string
- Marbles
- 1 small box

1 Cover the cereal boxes with colored paper. Decorate with shapes of mountains and trees.

2 Pierce a hole in the top of each box with a sharp pencil. Use modeling clay to push against.

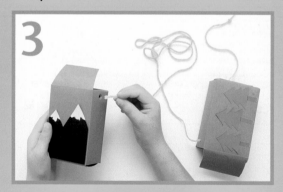

3 Thread the long piece of string through the holes as shown.

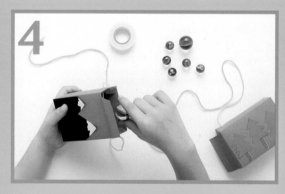

4 Place some marbles in each box, then tape the boxes shut.

5

6

Decorate the small box with colored paper to make it look like a cable car.

Tape the short piece of string to the car, and then tie it to the middle of the long piece of string.

Place the top station on a box. By pulling on the long piece of string, you can move your cable car from the station at the bottom up the mountain to the station at the top.

acid—a substance that can eat away other substances

adapted—changed over time

air—the mixture of gases that we breathe

buckle—to crumple and fold

cable—a long, thick rope usually made from metal wire

conifer—an evergreen tree that keeps its leaves all year long

crust—the hard, rocky surface of the Earth

deciduous tree—a tree that loses its leaves in the fall

down—soft, hairlike feathers that cover young birds

earthquake—the shaking of the ground caused by a sudden movement in the Earth's crust

elements—strong winds, heavy rain, and other kinds of bad weather

erupt—to explode, throwing ash, gas, and hot rock up into the air

experienced—describes people who have skills that they have developed over time

facilities—buildings and services, such as health care and schools

fossil—the remains of an ancient animal or plant found in rock

fuel—a substance burned to produce heat or power

glide—to move smoothly and quietly

gouge—to make a hole in something with force

hollow—a shallow hole

jagged—describes a surface that is sharp and uneven

lichen—a slow-growing plant that forms crusty branches on rocks, walls, and trees

oxygen—a common gas in the air that is necessary for human life

peak—the top part of a mountain

plate—a large area of land that "floats" on the liquid rock underneath

pollute—to make harmful waste that damages the environment

predict—to say what will happen in the future

ray—a beam of light that travels in a straight line

reflect—to bounce back from a surface

remote—describes an out-of-the-way place

resource—a raw material that can be used to make other things

rubble—a mixture of stones and rocks of different sizes

seabed—the land at the bottom of an ocean or sea

steel—a strong metal made from iron and carbon

suction—the process that occurs when two surfaces stick together because the air between them has been removed

terrace—a field with steps going down a hillside

vegetation—plant life

world-class—among the best in the world

The content of this book can be used to teach and reinforce various elements of the science and language arts curricula in the elementary grades. It also provides opportunities for crosscurricular lessons in math, geography, and art.

Extension activities

Writing and oral language
Images throughout this book show people participating in mountain sports or recreation. Choose an image that especially appeals to you and then research and write a one- or two-page report about that sport. Or you can research and write a one- or two-page biography of someone who has excelled at it. Share your writing in a presentation to others.

Creative writing
Imagine yourself as being the person in one of the images in this book. What is it like to be doing what you are doing? What led up to this point? Write a story describing your adventure.

Science
The study of mountains relates to the scientific themes of the structure and formation of Earth, Earth's history, and changes in and on Earth.

Some specific links to the science curriculum include adaptations (pp. 22–23, 24–25); conservation (pp. 30–31); engineering (pp. 28–29); habitats and ecosystems (pp. 14–15); natural disasters (pp. 8–9, 10–11, 38–39, 40–41); natural resources (pp. 32–33); plate tectonics (pp. 8–9, 10–11, 12–13); technology (pp. 34–35); weather and climate (pp. 16–17); and weathering and erosion (pp. 20–21).

Crosscurricular links
1) Geography/Math: The highest mountain peaks in the world are on the Asian continent, but every continent has its highest peak. Use references such as *http://geology. com/records/continents-highest-mountains.shtml* to find the locations, heights, and other information about the highest mountains on each continent. Create a graph comparing the

heights of these peaks.

2) Art/Science: Refer to the photos and drawing on pages 10–11 to help you build a model of a volcano. Put some baking soda (sodium bicarbonate) into a container and pour in vinegar (acetic acid) to make your volcano erupt.

Using the projects
Children can do these projects at home. Here are some ideas for extending them:

Page 44: Put the slabs side by side so they touch. Pull one slowly toward you and push the other one away. This is what happens when one piece of land slips past another and causes an earthquake.

Page 44: Divide the clay into four balls. Roll each one flat. Stack the clay in layers, alternating colors, like the diagram on page 12. Use a piece of string to cut the stack into three pieces and then build your own fault-block mountains.

Page 45: Mysterious beings and folklore characters are often portrayed as larger than life. Paul Bunyan is one such colorful character in American folklore. Read several of the many entertaining tales about him online. What kind of calling card could you make for him?

Page 46: A cable car system is designed not only to pull the car up the steep slope but also to keep it from going too fast back down. Experiment with downhill speed. Lean one end of a piece of wood or cardboard against a book to create a ramp with a slight slope. Place a marble at the top of the ramp and let go. Add more books, one at a time, each time releasing the marble. What do you notice as the slope gets steeper?

Did you know?

- Some mountain ranges are older than others. The Highlands in Scotland are 400 million years old, while the Alps in central Europe are only 15 million years old.

- The longest mountain range in the world is the Andes in South America. The mountains stretch for more than 4,300 mi. (7,000km).

- The slam of a car door, a falling branch, or the movement of a skier can all start an avalanche. Snow can speed down a mountain at 200 miles (320km) per hour!

- Glaciers store about 70 percent of the world's supply of fresh water and cover about ten percent of Earth's land.

- At the top of the Himalayas, fierce winds can reach more than 180 miles (300km) per hour.

- The highest altitude at which trees can grow is called the timberline. The highest timberline in the world is in the Bolivian Andes, where hardy trees can grow up to 17,000 ft. (5,200m) above sea level.

- K2 is the second-highest mountain on Earth after Everest. It is known as "Savage Mountain." One in five people who have tried to reach the top have died. Only 302 people have ever made it to the summit, compared to the 2,700 who have scaled Everest. K2 has never been climbed in the winter.

- Measured from the base, the tallest mountain is not Everest but Hawaii's Mauna Kea, which rises to a height of 31,200 ft. (9,500m) from the seabed.

- Because the temperature at the top of a mountain is much colder than at the bottom, it is possible to have snow at the equator, the warmest part of the world.

- The Himalayan jumping spider lives higher up than any other animal. At around 22,000 ft. (6,700m), its only food is insects blown by the wind from lower levels.

- The plates that folded up to form the Himalayas are still crashing into each other. Some mountains, such as Everest, continue to grow higher by about 0.4 in. (1cm) each year!

- Mount Stromboli, on a small Italian island, is one of the world's most active volcanoes. It has been erupting almost nonstop for the past 20,000 years!

- Mountain peoples and animals can live at great heights because they have bigger hearts and lungs, which carry more blood and oxygen.

- The world's highest-ever cable car system was located in the city of Mérida in Venezuela. It was more than 7 mi. (12km) long and reached a height of almost 15,800 ft. (4,800m).

- Tourism brings a lot of money for the people who live in the mountains. The Alps receives about 100 million visitors every year.

Mountains quiz

The answers to these questions can all be found by looking back through the book. See how many you get right. You can check your answers on page 56.

1) Which mountain range is home to the world's highest peaks?
A—Andes
B—Himalayas
C—Alps

2) When do mountains form?
A—When two plates push against each other
B—When two plates stay still
C—When two plates move away from each other

3) Where is air the thinnest on the mountains?
A—Down in valleys
B—At the top
C—Among pine trees

4) What is a large crack in a glacier called?
A—Lammergeier
B—Crevasse
C—Cirque

5) Which of these does not make rocks crumble?
A—Sunlight
B—Lichens
C—Glaciers

6) Why do farmers build terraces?
A—To separate different crops
B—To attract tourists
C—To stop the soil from washing away

7) Which of these is used to get up a mountain?
A—Cable car
B—Hang glider
C—Snowboard

8) What valuable material can be found in mountains?
A—Glass
B—Plastic
C—Metal

9) Reinhold Messner was the first person to climb Everest without . . .
A—A tent
B—Extra oxygen
C—Food

10) What breed of dog is used to sniff out the victims of avalanches?
A—Jack Russell terrier
B—St. Bernard
C—Beagle

11) Which can move downhill the quickest?
A—A glacier
B—An avalanche
C—A skier

12) Where is Bigfoot believed to live?
A—Kathmandu
B—Hawaiian Islands
C—Rocky Mountains

Books to read

Earth's Shifting Surface (Sci-Hi) by Robert Snedden, Heinemann-Raintree, 2010

The Himalayas (Mountains Around the World) by Molly Aloian, Crabtree, 2012

Inside Volcanoes by Melissa Stewart, Sterling, 2011

Mapping Mountains by Robert Walker, Marshall Cavendish, 2010

Mountain Animals (Saving Wildlife) by Sonya Newland, Smart Apple Media, 2012

Mountains Around the World (Geography Now!) by Jen Green, Rosen Publishing, 2009

True Mountain Rescue Stories by Glenn Scherer, Enslow, 2010

Places to visit

Alpine Visitor Center, Rocky Mountains National Park, Colorado

http://rockymountainnationalpark.com/ places/alpine_visitor_center.html

This visitor center is more than 11,480 ft. (3,500m) above sea level and has great views over the Rocky Mountains National Park. The park contains hundreds of miles of trails for hiking, horseback riding, or rock climbing. It is also one of the best places to see animals in the wild. Look out for coyotes, beavers, and bighorn sheep.

Loon Mountain, White Mountains, New Hampshire

www.loonmtn.com

The attractions at Loon mountain include a long, scenic gondola ride to the summit. At the top you can explore glacial caves, hike a nature trail, and climb the observation tower. Legend has it that there is lost gold in the caves!

American Museum of Natural History, New York

www.amnh.org

Inside this museum is the Hall of Planet Earth, which shows you how Earth and its oceans, continents, and mountains have evolved. It also explains how Earth is still shifting today to give us earthquakes and volcanoes. The earthquake monitoring station gives you the opportunity to monitor earthquake activity in real time.

Websites

www.mountainprofessor.com

This site explains how different types of mountains form and has pictures and descriptions of the highest mountains and most famous ranges in the world.

www.onegeology.org/eXtra/kids/ earthProcesses/glaciers.html

This website lets you explore Earth's processes. You can find out all about glaciers, including how they form, how they move, and how they melt.

http://vulcan.wr.usgs.gov/Outreach/ AboutVolcanoes/framework.html

Why do volcanoes occur? When will a volcano erupt? How hot is a volcano? Find out the answers to these and other questions on this site.

Mountains quiz answers

1) B	7) A
2) A	8) C
3) B	9) B
4) B	10) B
5) A	11) B
6) C	12) C